sideways   **around**

I'm pulling my friend along.

Move it!

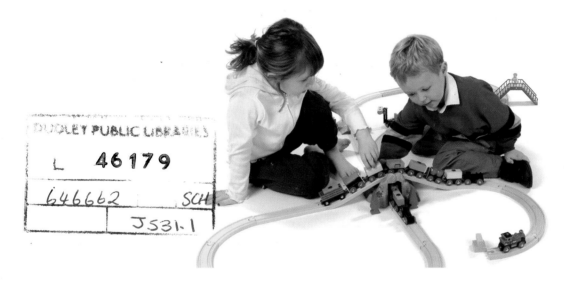

Julia Lawson
Photographs by
Peter Millard

Evans Brothers Limited

We can move our bodies in lots of different ways.

up

down

Now he's pushing me!

How would you like to go for a ride
Up in the air so blue?
We could go so high,
We could touch the sky.
We could fly! We could fly! We could fly!

We are trying to move our trains around the track. This engine is going through the tunnel.

This one is going up and over the hill, and this one is going under it!

My plane is made from paper. It can glide a long way.

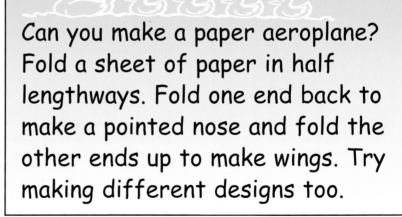

Can you make a paper aeroplane? Fold a sheet of paper in half lengthways. Fold one end back to make a pointed nose and fold the other ends up to make wings. Try making different designs too.

The eagle soars silently.

Our boats need wind to make them sail.

These boats have a propeller to make them go faster.

These leaves flutter slowly to the ground ...

... while the parachute floats gently down.

Make a parachute!
You need a plastic tub, some wool and a plastic bag. Attach four pieces of wool to the tub and tie the ends to a large piece of plastic. Watch it float down!

Did you know the cheetah is the fastest animal in the world ...

... and the tortoise is one of the slowest?

Pull ... tug ... heave!

Who is going to win the tug of war?

Notes and suggested activities for parents and teachers

We hope that you have enjoyed sharing this book and have tried out some of the additional ideas found in the activity boxes. Feel free to adapt them as you wish.

How things move is a theme that often fascinates children. An excellent way of developing this theme is to encourage the children to make models that move. Children can make 'junk' models or use some of the commercially produced packs. They could also collect some old mechanisms, take them apart and examine them closely, for example door handles, telephones or weighing scales. Listed below are some storybooks, action rhymes, videos and CD-Roms relating to the theme of movement. Have fun!

Storybooks
Wheels, Shirley Hughes, Walker Books
Duck in the Muck, Jez Alborough, Collins
Mrs Armitage on Wheels, Quentin Blake, Red Fox

Sports Day, Nick Butterworth & Mick Inkpen, Hodder
Fox on Wheels, James Marshall, Red Fox
Meg's Car, Helen Nicoll, Puffin
Aesop's Funky Fables 'The Hare and the Tortoise', Vivian French and Korky Paul, Hamish Hamilton

Action rhymes
This is a lovely action rhyme that the children can do with their hands:

Push Them, Pull Them
Push them, pull them, push them, pull them,
Give a little clap!
Raise them, lower them, raise them, lower them,
Put them in your lap!

Wave them, wiggle them, wave them, wiggle them,
Give a little shake!
Rub them, scrub them, rub them, scrub them,
Now let's have a break!

I'm a Little Aeroplane (to the tune of 'I'm a Little Teapot')
I'm a little aeroplane,
Watch me fly.
Like a silver bird,
Way up high.
First, I start my engines,
Then I fly.
Lifting off the runway,
Up into the sky.

Whisky Frisky
Whisky, frisky, hippity, hop,
Up we go, to the tree top.
Whirly, twirly, round and round,
Down we scamper, to the ground.
Creepy, crawly, slither and glide,
On our tums, we slip and slide!

Move It!
This is a fun variation of 'Simon Says'. Call out an action to the children, for example pushing, climbing, lifting or jumping, but the children are only meant to respond if the action is prefaced by your name. For example, 'Julia says, push up towards the sky'.

Musical Movements
Have a variety of instruments available, such as a drum, tambourine, triangle and a whistle, and use each one to signal a different movement. The beating of a drum could mean giant steps and a triangle could mean hopping. Play the instruments; the children must remember which movement goes with which instrument!

Videos
Percy the Park Keeper *The Rescue Party*, Hit Entertainment plc
Fourways Farm (series 1 and 2, includes stories introducing children to ideas on movement and forces), Channel 4
Stage One *Machines*, Channel 4

CD-Roms
The Tortoise and the Hare (Living Books), Broderbund
Bob the Builder *Can we Fix it?*, BBC Multimedia

Index

Photography acknowledgements
pages 11, 16, 17: Bruce Coleman Collection